WATERLOO LOCAL SCHOOL
PRIMARY LIBRARY

A GOLDEN WHEELS BOOK
Formula One
The Ultimate in Racing Cars

RICH TAYLOR

Photography by BILL OURSLER

GOLDEN PRESS / NEW YORK
Western Publishing Company, Inc., Racine, Wisconsin

Black-and-white photographs courtesy *Car and Driver*.
Diagram of Lotus 72 courtesy *Quattroruote,* Milan.

Library of Congress Catalog Card Number: 74-77912

Copyright © 1974 by Western Publishing Company, Inc. All rights reserved. Printed in the U.S.A. Golden, a Golden Book® and Golden Press® are trademarks of Western Publishing Company, Inc.

Second Printing, 1975

Grand Prix Racing

The first Grand Prix race was held in 1906 near Le Mans, France. This was only twelve years after the first organized competition between motor vehicles, a rudimentary reliability trial between Paris and Rouen. Sponsored by l'Automobile Club de France, the Grand Prix was intended to compete with the Gordon Bennett series begun in 1899 by James Gordon Bennett, publisher of the *New York Herald*. The ACF regulations specified a maximum weight of 1000kg (2204 lbs.) and allowed only the driver and his riding mechanic to work on the car once the race had begun.

Most competitors entered monster vehicles having more than 12-liter engines. The largest of these leviathans was a four-cylinder Panhard of 18,279cc; each cylinder held one and a half times the displacement of an entire current Formula One engine, and the piston tops were the size of pie plates. The thirty-two giant cars that appeared on race day were expected to cover twelve laps of a 64-mile course—six laps one day, six the next. Most of the machines suffered mechanical failures. Of the few that finished, the leading survivor was Francois Szisz, driving a huge Renault, who covered the course at an average speed of almost 63 miles per hour.

Immediately, the race organizers began a dizzying series of rules changes, most of them aimed at reducing the terrifying top speeds of over 100 miles per hour that the primitive cars were already capable of reaching. In 1907, regulations remarkably similar to modern Grand Prix rules were put into effect in Europe. For the Kaiserpreise—the German equivalent of the French Grand Prix—engine displacement was restricted to a maximum of 8-liters. A maximum fuel consumption of 9.4 miles per gallon was allowed for the second Grand Prix in France, which the organizers hoped would likewise favor smaller and theoretically slower cars.

Racing colors to signify the country of origin—British Racing Green, French Blue, Italian Racing Red—were adopted from the Gordon Bennett. These became the international rule for sixty years, until nationalistic loyalties were displaced and the cars turned into mobile billboards representing sponsors and advertisers.

In 1908, further rules changes were made. A minimum weight of 2425 lbs. and maximum engine size of approximately 13-liters were combined in a new international formula. This was first tried in the French Grand Prix at Dieppe, and limited top speeds to about 105 mph—on gravel and dirt roads, in powerful cars with insufficient tires, two-wheel brakes and no safety equipment at all. Not surprisingly, the first fatality in a Grand Prix occurred at Dieppe, and racing under the international formula was banned until 1912. It was then revived by the ACF.

The race-winning Peugeot in 1912 had a 7603cc four-cylinder engine with shaft-driven double overhead camshafts, central spark plugs, hemispherical combustion chambers and four valves per cylinder. Virtually every subsequent racing engine has been based in some way on this revolutionary design—a true turning point in the history of the internal combustion engine.

In 1913, the Grand Prix was won by an even smaller Peugeot of only 5.6-liters, followed by a sister car and a 3-liter Sunbeam. The success of these smaller cars prompted the ACF to reduce the maximum engine capacity to 4.5-liters, at the same time retaining the 2425 lb. minimum weight for the 1914 French Grand Prix. The Mercedes team finished one-two-three in immaculate and classic racers after an epic race-long duel with Frenchman Georges Boillot at the wheel of a Peugeot. At the time, it was taken by many as a portent of events to come in the even greater contest of nations already brewing.

World War I broke out within the month, and European racing disappeared until 1919, when a few amateur events were held.

The most successful racing car in the period just before World War I was the Grand Prix Peugeot designed by Ernest Henry, seen here at the 1913 Indianapolis 500.

Golden Era of the Twenties

The French Grand Prix was revived in 1921, along with a similar Italian event. Both were run to the same formula as the Indianapolis 500—3-liter engines in 1763-lb. chassis. Jimmy Murphy won the Gallic race in a Duesenberg—the first victory for an American driver in an American car in a major European race. It was also the last until the success of Dan Gurney and the nominally All American Eagle at the Belgian Grand Prix nearly a half-century later, in 1967.

For 1922, the Grand Prix formula was reduced again, this time to 2-liters, with a minimum weight of 1433 lbs. A popular set of rules, even though they survived for only four years, the 2-liter formula accounted for some of the most interesting of all Grand Prix cars. The legendary Alfa Romeo P2 designed by Vittorio Jano dominated the series, but the most

The Type 35 and Type 37 Bugattis are among the most beautiful racing cars ever built, although even when they first appeared in 1923 they weren't powerful enough to be winners in international competition.

elegant—though uncompetitive—car was undoubtedly the lovely Bugatti Type 35. For the same formula, Ernest Henry designed the classic Sunbeam Fours with double overhead cams and 16 valves, while Fiat produced its classic Types 804 and 805.

Supercharging arrived in 1923 on a 130-hp version of the Fiat 805. Mercedes also produced a supercharged version, claimed to develop 160 hp. In the few short years of the 2-liter era, horsepower figures doubled, engine speeds increased significantly, exotic fuels were developed and superchargers became required equipment. As a period of intense technological advancement, it hasn't been equaled in any succeeding period.

Alfa Romeo built the superlatively engineered P3 in 1932. It was one of the earliest Grand Prix cars with no accommodation for a riding mechanic.

The Grand Prix formula was reduced once more in 1926, this time to tiny 1.5-liter engines in 1322-lb. cars. After only two years of this formula, Grands Prix suffered a decline brought about partly by the Depression and partly by a rising interest in sports car and long-distance racing. However, in 1932 the Association Internationale des Automobile Clubs Reconnus—which had regulated racing since 1922—instituted another formula allowing single-seat racing cars of unlimited displacement.

The first new *monoposto* was the Alfa Romeo P3 —one of the most significant Grand Prix cars ever built, and the absolute masterpiece of Vittorio Jano. This used a 2.65-liter Straight-8 to develop 180 hp, fitted to a 1500-lb. car. Similar but less puissant Monza Alfas were raced the following year without direct factory involvement by Scuderia Ferrari, whose principal competition came from Type 51 Bugattis, and later the exquisitely engineered 3.2-liter, 240-hp Type 59s.

For 1934, the Grand Prix formula was again altered slightly. A maximum weight of 1653 lbs. was established, together with a minimum race length of 500km, or 310 miles. The Bugatti Type 59 fitted the formula—as did the P3 Alfa—but they were both completely overshadowed by revolutionary Auto Union and Mercedes-Benz factory cars, financially backed by the new Nazi regime and specifically intended as Aryan world-beaters.

The Auto Union, designed by Ferdinand Porsche, was the more radical of the two. Its mid-engine was positioned behind the driver, the frame had tubular members and the suspension was all-independent. The engine was an intricate 4360cc V-16, with a single overworked camshaft operating all 32 valves. It was claimed to produce 295 hp.

The comparatively conventional front-engine Mercedes also used independent suspension all around, hydraulic brakes and a supercharged 3360cc, double overhead cam Straight-8 rated at 390 hp. By the last year of the formula in 1937, the Mercedes displaced 5660cc and developed 640 hp. These were easily the most powerful Grand Prix cars ever built, and only within the last few years of the unlimited displacement Can-Am has anyone fielded a road racing car with anywhere near the same horsepower.

In an attempt to curtail the German machines, the French AIACR in 1938 limited supercharged cars to 3-liters and normally aspirated cars to 4.5-liters. This was accompanied by a sliding scale equating weight to displacement. Supercharged cars from Germany still retained the advantage, however, with Mercedes and Auto Union creating similar 3-liter V-12s, both of which were rated at 485 hp just before World War II erupted.

The FIA and a True Formula One

The French were the first to reorganize following the war, holding a Grand Prix race in the Paris suburban park of the Bois de Boulogne just three months after the cessation of hostilities. Various prewar cars were raced until the first postwar formula went into effect in 1948, following the reorganization of the AIACR into the Fédération Internationale de l'Automobile. Racing was put under the jurisdiction of the Commission Sportive Internationale, a committee of the FIA. The CSI proposed a Formula One of 1.5-liters supercharged or 4.5-liters unsupercharged. They also recommended a Formula Two for unsupercharged 2-liter cars and a Formula Three for unsupercharged 500cc miniature racers.

In 1950, the World Championship of Drivers was initiated, specifying six races in which competitors could collect points leading to an overall series championship. The major contenders were the supercharged 1.5-liter Alfa Romeo 158s. Ranged against them were 4.5-liter Ferraris, Maseratis, Lago-Talbots and the abortive BRM 1.5-liter V-16. Races were run in Belgium, France, Monaco, Switzerland

By 1939, Mercedes-Benz had dominated racing for five years; the ultimate development was this Type W163, a supercharged V-12 of nearly 500 hp.

and Italy. An International Trophy was also held at Silverstone, England. Giuseppe Farina became the first World Champion in an Alfa 158. Juan Fangio was the runner-up in another Alfa. Fangio won the first of his five World Championships in a similar Alfa 159 the following year.

Alfa withdrew from racing in 1952, and most other teams decided to concentrate on the 2-liter Formula Two. The inevitable result was that the FIA turned Formula Two into the championship series—in effect, a 2-liter Formula One.

Despite the appearance of numerous British HWMs, Coopers, Connaughts and Frazer-Nashes, some Gordinis from France and OSCAs and Maseratis from Italy, the World Champion, Alberto Ascari, drove a Ferrari Tipo 500 to victory in six of the seven Grands Prix in 1952. His teammate, Piero Taruffi, won the other. Ferrari drivers Ascari, Farina and Taruffi finished one-two-three in the season standings, and Ascari repeated as World Champion in the same car the next year.

In 1954 a new formula, which was to survive through 1960, was introduced. This specified a 2.5-liter unsupercharged engine with no weight restrictions, coupled with a minimum race distance of 186 miles. The leaders of the formula were expected to be enlarged versions of the successful 2-liter Ferraris. To challenge Ferrari, Maserati built one of the last classic Grand Prix cars—the famous 250F—with a tubular space frame, coil spring independent front suspension, De Dion rear axle and a 240-hp double overhead cam Six developed from a 2-liter Formula Two powerplant designed by Gioacchino Colombo.

Juan Manuel Fangio, probably the greatest pilot in racing history, drove a Mercedes-Benz W196 to World Championships in 1954 and 1955.

Vittorio Jano, famous for his classic P2 and P3 Alfas, designed a new car for Lancia. This also used a tubular space frame, independent front suspension and De Dion rear, and produced 260 hp. The most intriguing features of the Lancia were outboard fuel and oil tanks rigged into sponsons in line with the wheels. Other cars were Gordini, HWM, Connaught and Vanwall—but, as it turned out, all were merely supporting actors for the triumphant return of Mercedes-Benz to Grand Prix racing.

Return of Mercedes-Benz

It was precisely forty years since Mercedes had astonished the French at the 1914 "Greatest Grand Prix," and precisely twenty years since the awesome Mercedes W25 had signaled the beginning of Nazi road-racing domination. The Mercedes W196, with a 290-hp Straight-8, desmodromic valve gear, independent suspension on all four wheels, inboard

Fangio won his fifth World Championship in a Maserati 250F in 1957, after which both he and Maserati retired from Grand Prix competition.

brakes and full streamlining, appeared for the French Grand Prix. The team finished one-two and lapped the entire field. Winner Juan Fangio went on to give himself and Mercedes a decisive World Championship for the 1954 season.

Fangio repeated in the tragically abbreviated 1955 season. In June of that year, an eccentric driver named Bouillon, racing as "Pierre Levegh," crashed into the crowd at Le Mans, killing himself and more than eighty spectators. This precipitated a wave of unparalleled anti-racing legislation. The Grands Prix of France, Germany, Spain and Switzerland were cancelled, no further French races of any sort were run that summer, Switzerland banned racing permanently and Mercedes-Benz retired as World Champions for the third time in four decades.

In 1959, Coopers won five of eight Grand Prix races; Stirling Moss, shown here, maintained his reputation as Fangio's successor, even though Jack Brabham took the championship that year.

The retirement of Mercedes signaled a new era in Formula One development. Ferrari took over the Jano-designed Lancia D50, adding horsepower and removing the side-mounted fuel sponsons. The resultant Lancia-Ferrari was competitive with refined Maserati 250Fs. A revised British Vanwall sponsored by Tony Vandervell appeared—with chassis designed by Colin Chapman and body by Frank Costin. BRM finally got a 2.5-liter car to the grid, but it was fragile and uncompetitive. While others refined their new designs, the well-sorted Ferrari of Fangio took him to a fourth World Championship in 1956 over Stirling Moss in a Maserati.

Mid-engine Revolution

The 1957 season was again dominated by Fangio, this time in his own Maserati 250F which took him to his last Grand Prix championship. However, observant spectators knew that the real significance rode with a relatively unknown Australian driver named Jack Brabham. He scored championship points in a mid-engine British Formula Two Cooper fitted with a Coventry Climax four-cylinder portable fire pump engine. The engine had been enlarged to 1.9-liters but developed a mere 175 hp. This was insignificant by comparison with the 270 hp of the powerful Vanwalls and Maseratis that set the pace.

The light and agile Cooper needed only more power to be fully competitive. In 1958, the Cooper's displacement was raised to 2.2-liters and two championship races were won. However, the battle was now between Ferrari and Vanwall, with the Italian red Dino 246 taking Mike Hawthorn to the Drivers Championship and British Racing Green triumphing in the newly created simultaneous series for Formula One manufacturers. Stirling Moss, whose brilliant racing career included many years of Grand Prix competition—in which he earned four second-place seasons and three thirds—lost the championship to Hawthorn by one point. Hawthorn gained the point for Ferrari when he set the fastest lap in the Portuguese Grand Prix won by Moss, in a Vanwall.

In 1959 Vanwall retired and Ferrari persisted with a front-engine chassis. The Cooper now used a full-capacity 2.5-liter Coventry Climax, and although it gave only about 240 hp—some fifty less than the Ferrari—there was much less Cooper to propel. Coopers won five of the eight Grands Prix run in 1959, with Jack Brabham acquiring his first World Championship. His second came in 1960, again with the Cooper.

The Commission Sportive Internationale once more determined to reduce racing speeds. For 1961, just as in 1952, the previous Formula Two became the championship series. A minimum weight of 992 lbs. was specified for the 1.5-liter cars. And, for the first time, rollbars were required.

The British protested the rules change, lost valuable development time and were reduced to running uprated versions of Formula Two cars. Most of these had Coventry Climax FPF Fours, good for no more than 150 hp. Ferrari, however, introduced a completely new car powered by a double overhead cam V-6, rated at 190 hp. By mid-season, a Coventry Climax V-8 with 170 hp was available in Britain, and a similar BRM unit appeared before autumn, but neither was a threat to the winning Ferrari of American Phil Hill.

Ferrari encountered internal personnel problems during the winter of 1962. The better part of its racing department quit, leaving the field to BRM,

The Lotus 25 was competitive for four seasons; this is Peter Arundell heading for a third-place finish in the 1964 Dutch Grand Prix at Zandvoort.

Cooper, Lotus, Lola and the driver-built Brabhams of the former two-time World Champion. Porsche introduced a moderately successful air-cooled Flat-8 with double overhead cams and 185 hp. But the big news in 1962 was the Lotus 25, the first successful monocoque chassis.

The Lotus Monocoque and Jim Clark

Jim Clark's Lotus 25 dominated the year, although Graham Hill won the championship for BRM after a mechanical failure put Clark out while leading the last race of the season in South Africa. In 1963, however, Clark won seven of the ten races, with one second and one third. He failed to finish only once. He and Lotus were awarded the championship for one of the best single seasons achieved by a driver in modern Grand Prix racing.

Most cars remained basically unchanged for 1964, although Ferrari introduced a fuel-injected V-8 which produced 215 hp—compared to the 195 hp of the Coventry Climax and 200 hp of the BRM. In mid-season the first Honda V-12 appeared. This had four valves per cylinder, double overhead cams and no fewer than twelve carburetors. It was claimed to give 225 hp from 1500cc, at a dizzy 13,000 rpm. The summer was divided among Clark, Hill and John Surtees, with the latter's Ferrari taking the championship in the final race of the season after the retirement of the other two. Clark came back to win for Lotus in 1965, however, in the last year of the 1.5-liter formula.

Unlike the 4.5-liter formula of the early Fifties, which faded away from disinterest, the 1.5-liter formula saw some of the best racing in history. Technological progress had been so remarkable that the tiny racers were faster around a given course than any in the past—including the gargantuan German machines of the late Thirties, which boasted three times the power. The 1.5-liter formula was much mourned, but the prospect of greater horsepower from engines of double the capacity was enough to make the change to 3-liter engines in 1102-lb. cars (later upped to 1265 lbs.) welcomed in most circles.

The well-engineered Ferraris were expected to control the 1966 season, for these had a proven 330-hp V-12—borrowed from the firm's sports cars—in conservative semi-monocoque chassis. As it turned out, however, Ferrari was merely another contender. Others in the running were the Cooper, powered by an enlarged version of a V-12 that Maserati had prepared in 1957 for the end of the 2.5-liter formula; BRM's overly intricate H-16, composed of two Flat-8s mounted one above the other and geared together; Lotus's inadequate cars, powered by either 2-liter Coventry Climax V-8 or BRM H-16 engines; McLaren's first racers, with unreliable versions of the Ford V-8 intended for Indianapolis; the chronically overweight Honda V-12, which appeared for the last race of the season; and the hard-luck Dan Gurney AAR Eagle, which spent the season waiting for a promised V-12 designed by Harry Weslake.

The hero of 1966 was Jack Brabham. Unlike his technologically advanced Coopers of 1959 and '60, his first Brabhams—powered by 3-liter Repco single overhead cam V-8s based on Oldsmobile F-85 passenger car engines—were the epitome of conservative engineering. At Rheims, Brabham won. It was the first Grand Prix victory by a driver in a car bearing his own name. He then went on to take the World Championship. Despite increasing opposition as other teams sorted out their cars, his teammate Denis Hulme repeated for Brabham in 1967.

The Ford Cosworth DFV

If there was a moment of singular importance during the 3-liter formula, it came when a Lotus 49, designed by Maurice Phillippe, appeared at the Dutch Grand Prix with a new engine created by British engineer Keith Duckworth and financed by the Ford Motor Company. This was the Ford Cosworth DFV, a rather straightforward double overhead cam V-8 rated at 400 hp in its first appearance.

Most of 1967 was spent in sorting the new car and engine, and at the end of the season Ford management made an ultimately momentous decision to sell Ford Cosworth DFVs to other Grand Prix teams.

Few changes occurred in 1968. Matra appeared with cars for Jackie Stewart under the auspices of Ken Tyrrell, and one was promptly fitted with a Ford Cosworth. BRM had a new monocoque for a developed V-12, but it was expected to be Jimmy Clark's year in a Lotus. As predicted, Clark won the South African Grand Prix at the beginning of the season

Rob Walker's independent Lotus 49, driven by Jo Siffert at Brands Hatch in 1968, shows an early version of the Ford Cosworth and rudimentary wings at front and rear. The airfoils were later banned as unsafe.

(surpassing Fangio's record as he scored his twenty-fifth victory), but then died tragically in a minor Formula Two race at Hockenheim, Germany. A distraught Graham Hill was left to soldier on to the championship for Lotus.

Technologically, another revolution was at hand with the application of relatively sophisticated aero-

In 1971, Jackie Stewart won his second of three World Championships in a Tyrrell. He is seen here competing in the Spanish Grand Prix in April of that year.

dynamics to Grand Prix cars. The fad for inverted airfoils to exert downpressure on chassis and suspensions for greater roadholding spread to every Grand Prix team. Because of hasty construction, many of these were dangerous supplements to otherwise rational designs. A number of accidents were caused by the wings, with the result that emergency changes in the formula were written to exclude the devices.

Attempts to circumvent these prohibitions dominated the following wave of designs. There was also a brief interest in four-wheel-drive, but this dissipated quickly in the face of comparable performance gains achieved by the much simpler and less expensive wings, ducts, fins and airfoils with which the cars bristled.

The combine of Stewart/Tyrrell/Matra finally clicked in 1969, giving the Scot his first of three World Championships and Matra its first and last. The following year was one of significant change. Robin Herd designed the Ford Cosworth March, and the Ford Cosworth Tyrrell appeared late in the season. John Surtees also came to the grid under Ford Cosworth power in a car of his own manufacture. Frank Williams allied himself and his driver, Piers Courage, with the consistently disappointing products of Alejandro De Tomaso. The first V-12 all-Matra was built, along with an Alfa Romeo V-8 shoehorned into a McLaren chassis. The Ferrari 312 was finally developed into a serious contender, as was the BRM V-12. And the first monocoque Brabham was designed by Ron Tauranac.

The real innovation of 1970, however, was the brilliant Lotus 72 by Maurice Phillippe, which carried Jochen Rindt to four successive victories and Grand Prix racing's first posthumous World Championship. In that same unhappy year Bruce McLaren and Piers Courage were also killed.

In 1971, most constructors contented themselves with changes to the previous year's chassis, although a new March 711 patterned on the Lotus 72 came from Robin Herd. The refined Tyrrell of Jackie Stewart won the championship—the fourth consecutive year that Ford Cosworths dominated Grands Prix. The following season was notable for the repeat success of the Lotus 72, bringing Brazilian Emerson Fittipaldi the championship over favorite Jackie Stewart, who spent the season sorting out a new Tyrrell monocoque.

For his retirement season of 1973, Stewart had things pretty much his own way, marred only by the death of his Tyrrell teammate and apprentice, Francois Cevert, at the last race of the season in Watkins Glen. The only new cars of significance were the Shadows of Don Nichols and the Ensign designed by Mo Nunn, two of the many Ford Cosworth contenders that fleshed out Grand Prix grids. The curiously inept Techno team was never able to get itself sufficiently organized to provide the hapless Chris Amon with a competitive car, and Dan Gurney's avowed return to Grand Prix racing with a Ford Cosworth-powered Eagle never materialized.

A Look to the Future

The 3-liter formula seems destined to run at least until 1976, and whether the CSI will once again change the rules or whether these popular cars will be kept is impossible to forecast. Certainly the current Grand Prix formula has been the most successful in history, and perhaps the most stable as well. Formula One has never prospered in stability, however, and the easy availability of the overwhelming Ford Cosworths has fostered a tendency toward the moribund. No new engine is predicted to break the current stranglehold, making it anyone's guess as to the direction the CSI will take to spark the technological development so necessary to the continued vitality and success of Formula One racing. □

By August of 1971, at the Nürburgring Grand Prix, Stewart's Tyrrell had sprouted a new full-width nose, courtesy of designer Derek Gardner, and a ram air box for the Ford Cosworth engine.

Typical Formula One Car
The 3-liter Lotus 72

Rubber-lined fuel cells on each side severely limit the driver's space. These are located between the axles for minimum change in weight distribution as they empty during a race. The driver reclines on a lightly padded sheet of alloy, with the leather-covered wheel at full arms length. He is strapped in position by belts at shoulders, waist and thighs.

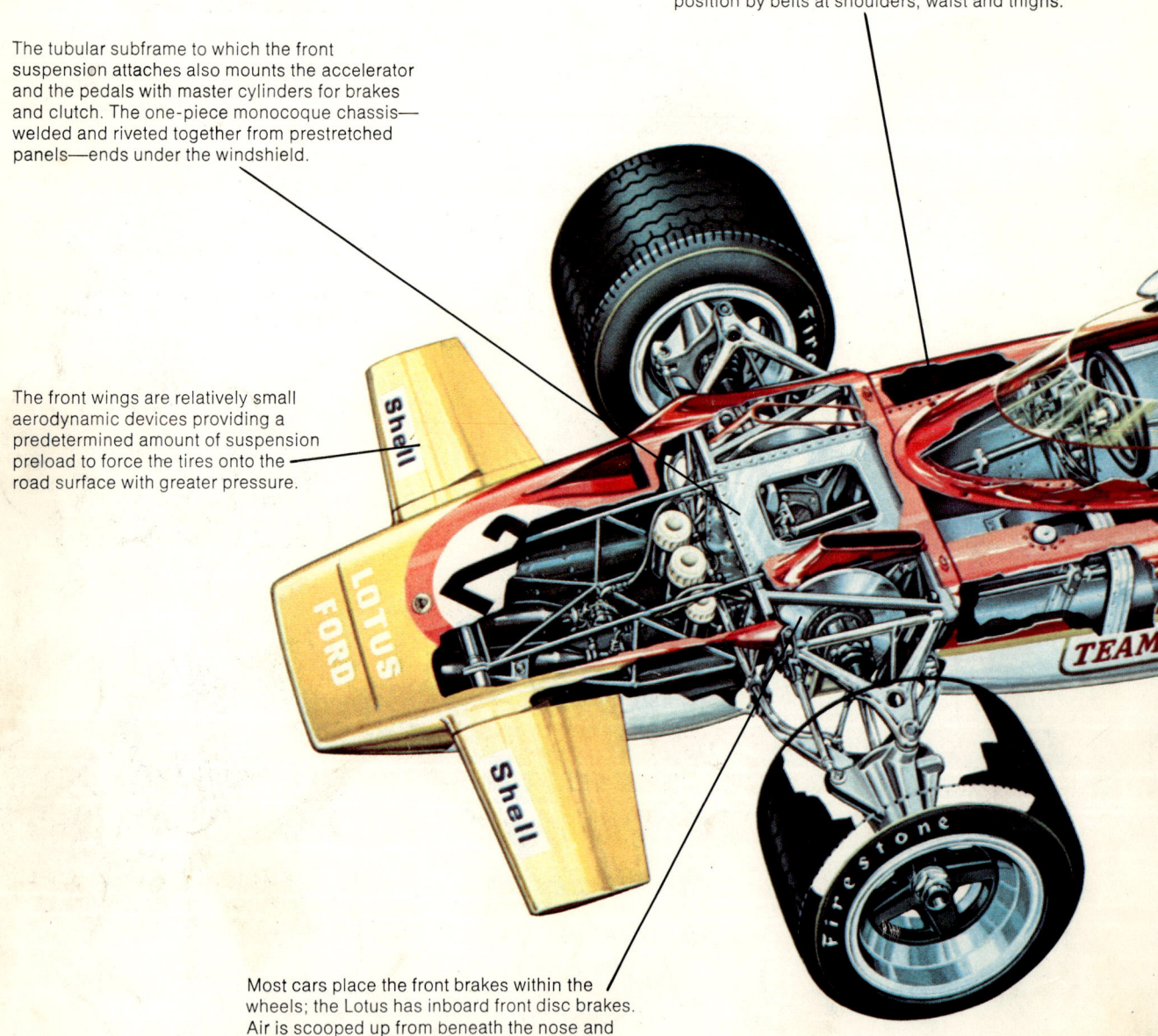

The tubular subframe to which the front suspension attaches also mounts the accelerator and the pedals with master cylinders for brakes and clutch. The one-piece monocoque chassis—welded and riveted together from prestretched panels—ends under the windshield.

The front wings are relatively small aerodynamic devices providing a predetermined amount of suspension preload to force the tires onto the road surface with greater pressure.

Most cars place the front brakes within the wheels; the Lotus has inboard front disc brakes. Air is scooped up from beneath the nose and exhausted through elevated slots in the upper body surface. The whirling of the discs aids in the ram effect of the cooling air.

796.1

WATERLOO LOCAL SCHOOL
PRIMARY LIBRARY

Seemingly insubstantial, the rollbar can support the 1500-lb. car many times over. The monocoque ends at this point, providing great torsional rigidity because of its short length-to-width ratio. The engine bolts directly to the rear of the monocoque; the rear suspension is mounted to the engine. The powerplant is thus a load-bearing part of the chassis.

Most cars use a single rear wing to apply downforce to the chassis for greater cornering ability. The Lotus wing is uniquely divided into three separate airfoils, each with a different angle of attack.

The Hewland transaxle mounts to the rear of the engine. The half-shafts, inboard disc brakes, remote oil sump and, in some cars, the wing mount directly to the transaxle.

Since the Ford Cosworth has a dry sump, the oil supply rides in its own tank behind the transaxle. This is fitted with a side-mounted radiator for increased cooling.

Water radiators for the engine, mounted to the rear of the monocoque, flank the driver. The large scoops ram cooling air through grilles protecting the delicate radiators from flying debris.

Wide cast alloy wheels with center-mount knock-off hubs attach to forged carriers. These in turn connect to the subframe with fabricated wishbones. Anti-sway bars stretch across the chassis at both front and rear. The Lotus is unique in its use of torsion bars. All other racers are fitted with conventional coil spring/shock absorbers.

Compact and sturdy, the Ford Cosworth is one of the most versatile Grand Prix engines ever designed. The Lotus 72 has subsequently been fitted with a huge air box to give a ram effect to air entering the fuel-metering units. The curling headers exit into four-into-one collectors.

Brabham

Although the name remains, the present Brabham team has nothing to do with Australian Jack Brabham. Brabham retired in 1971 after a fantastically successful driving career spanning two decades, during which he was three times World Champion. He was also the first successful builder/owner/driver in modern times, producing his first Formula One car in 1962. All Brabhams since then have been technically conservative racers, retaining conventional tubular space frames, for example, years after other constructors had switched to more advanced one-piece monocoque chassis. Nevertheless, Brabhams have always been sturdy cars with an excellent reputation.

Much of the success of the early 3-liter cars that achieved World Championships in 1966 and 1967 was due to Ron Tauranac, the Australian designer whose skills meshed happily with the car development ability of Jack Brabham himself. The present organization was originally purchased from Brabham by Tauranac and

Type: BT42 **Engine:** Ford Cosworth DFV, V-8 85.6x64.8mm, 2993cc; 450 hp at 9500 rpm **Transmission:** Hewland FG400A 5-speed transaxle **Chassis:** Monocoque **Wheelbase:** 94 in **Length:** 167 in **Width:** 75 in **Height:** 36 in **Track, F/R:** 57.5/57.0 in **Weight:** 1265 lbs **Wheels, F/R:** 11x13-in/14x13-in **Tires, F/R:** 10x20/17x26, Goodyear **Suspension, F/R:** Upper and lower wishbones, outboard coil spring/shock absorbers/Twin radius arms, single upper links, double lower links, outboard coil spring/shock absorbers **Brakes, F/R:** Outboard disc/Inboard disc, Girling **Fuel capacity:** 43 gal

Bernie Ecclestone. The next season Motor Racing Developments, which Ecclestone controls, succeeded to full ownership when Tauranac left to join Frank Williams' Iso Marlboro team.

The current car looks unusual, with a triangular monocoque projecting noticeably just ahead of the rear wheels. Twin radiators are hidden behind the wide, louvered nosepiece. The wheelbase is very short and, because of the ground-scraping monocoque, fuel loads are carried very low. Aside from the rather odd configuration of the body panels and monocoque, however, the car is utterly conventional in design and construction. It would seem to be a competent basis for a winning car, needing only a bit of expert sorting out to be competitive. But such testing so far has been beyond the capabilities of Motor Racing Developments, and without the services of Brabham and Tauranac, Ecclestone's team has unfortunately suffered some truly mediocre seasons.

BRM

BRM began as a showcase for the British automobile industry after World War II, but failed miserably in Grand Prix competition and was bought up by the Owen Group in 1953. It retains much of its nationalistic character, however, soldiering bravely on for nearly a quarter of a century while only once winning a World Championship (in 1962). Never really slow enough to be considered hopeless, BRM products have rarely risen to competitive status.

The best years for BRM have been those when it has either bought engines from someone else, or built its own relatively simple designs. But the propensity at Bourne has been to over-engineer powerplants, from the incredible supercharged 1.5-liter V-16 with which BRM began to the abortive 3-liter H-16 which preceded the present ineffective V-12.

It is an unfortunate truth that while the presence of BRM and Ferrari is the only thing keeping Formula One from turning into a boring one-engine class, BRM certainly would be better off scrapping the V-12 and buying engines from Cosworth. Aside from the deformable impact structure surrounding the cockpit—added at the beginning of the 1973 season—the current BRM is largely as raced since 1971. This car, in turn, is based closely on Tony Southgate's previous P153 BRM, designed for the 1970 season.

The present car is characterized by a rather bulbous monocoque, with much smoother contours through the cockpit section than the competition. A Tyrrell-type nose with stabilizing wings is fitted at the front, while a huge horizontal wing with equally large vertical fins dangles off the stern. The car is quite squat through the cockpit, and the driver sits uncommonly low. The small air box covers the top of the long V-12, and side ducting for engine and brake cooling extends to the very forward edge of the huge rear tires. The engine itself is left largely exposed, however.

The conventional chassis seems to work very well, the current problem seeming to be a dearth of superior driving talent to compensate for insufficient horsepower. A large team has often taken to the grid, with the inevitable result that the cars are not always as well prepared as they might be. However, the real source of BRM's problems continues to reside in the engine compartment.

Type: P160E **Engine:** BRM 142, V-12 74.6x57.2mm, 2999cc; 440 hp at 10,750 rpm **Transmission:** BRM 161 5-speed transaxle **Chassis:** Monocoque **Wheelbase:** 97.6 in **Length:** 180 in **Width:** 79 in **Height:** 32 in **Track, F/R:** 58.0/62.0 in **Weight:** 1265 lbs **Wheels, F/R:** 10x13-in/17x13-in **Tires, F/R:** 10x20/17x26, Firestone **Suspension, F/R:** Upper and lower wishbones, outboard coil spring/ shock absorbers/Twin radius arms, single upper links, lower wishbones, outboard coil spring/shock absorbers **Brakes, F/R:** Outboard disc/Inboard disc, Lockheed **Fuel Capacity:** 43 gal

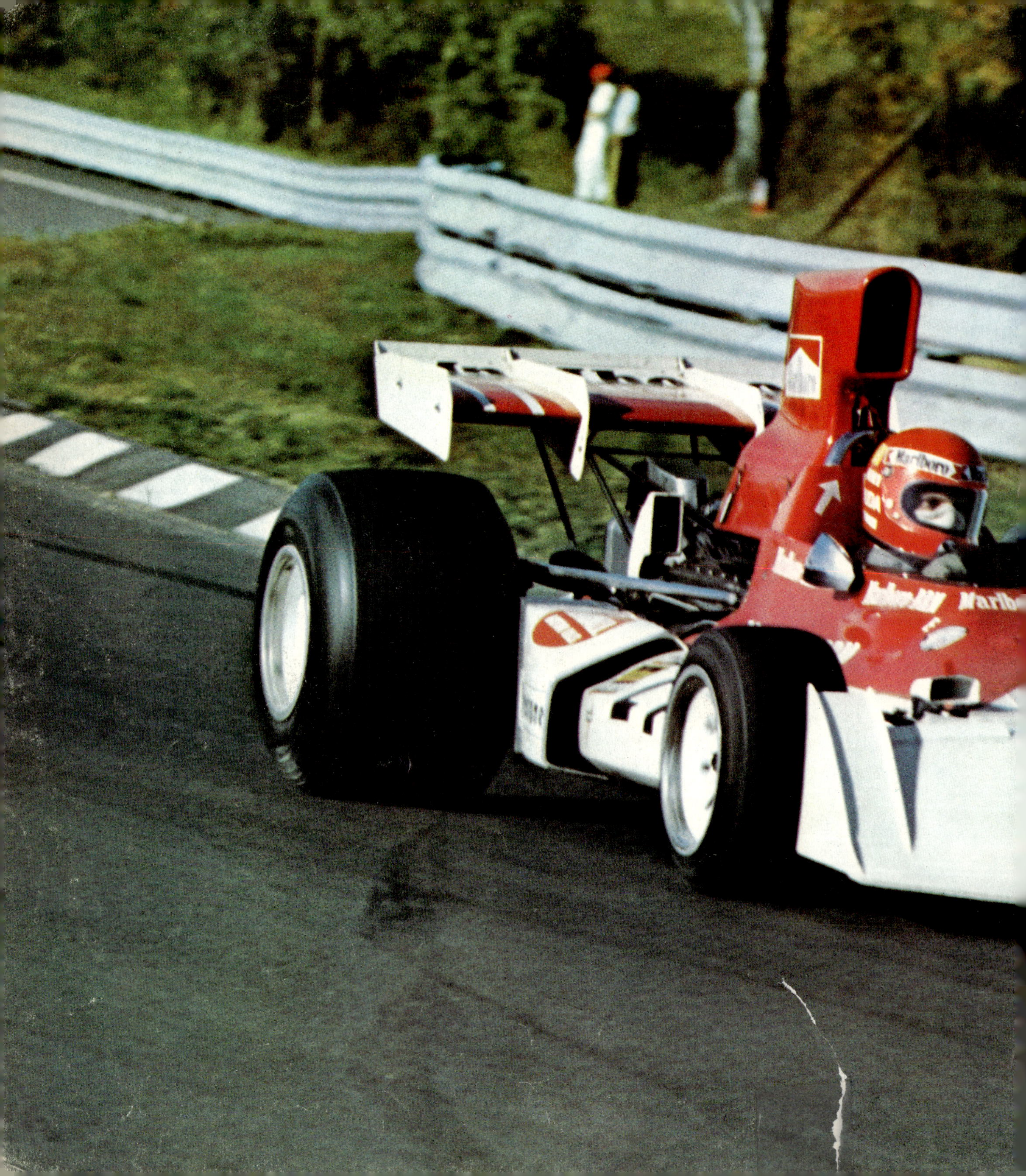

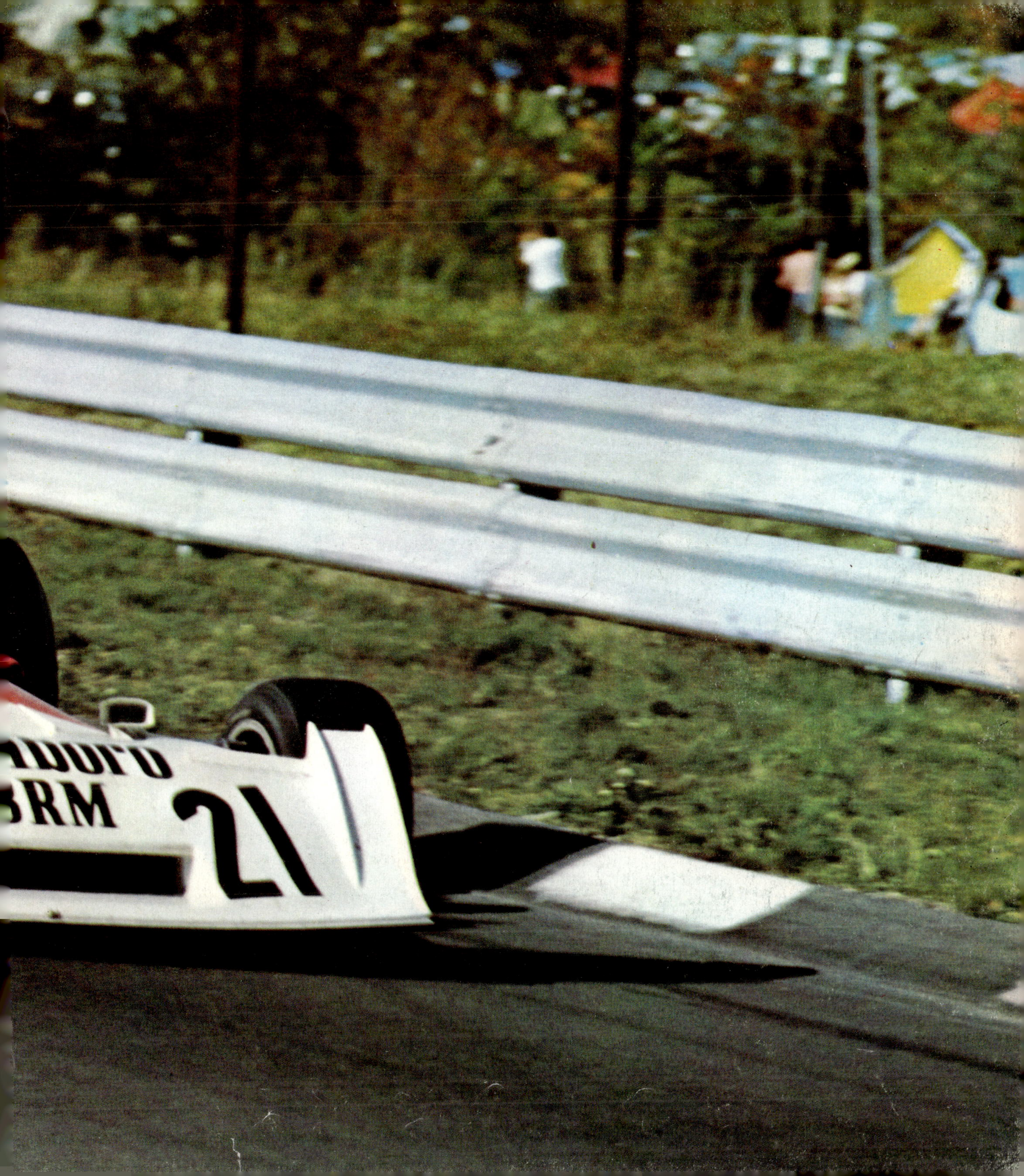
21

Type: MN **Engine:** Ford Cosworth DFV, V-8 85.6x64.8mm, 2993cc; 450 hp at 10,000 rpm
Transmission: Hewland FG400A 5-speed transaxle **Chassis:** Monocoque
Wheelbase: 95 in **Length:** 178 in
Width: 77 in **Height:** 40 in
Track, F/R: 61.0/60.0 in **Weight:** 1270 lbs
Wheels, F/R: 11x13-in/17x13-in
Tires, F/R: 10x20/16x26, Firestone
Suspension, F/R: Upper and lower wishbones, outboard coil spring/shock absorbers/Twin radius arms, single upper links, double lower links, outboard coil spring/shock absorbers
Brakes, F/R: Outboard disc/Inboard disc, Girling **Fuel Capacity:** 42 gal

Ensign

Ensign was a tiny British manufacturer of Formula Three cars—not unlike dozens of others—until abruptly elevated into Formula One in 1973 with the financial backing of driver Rikky von Opel. Von Opel is the grandson of Adam Opel, founder of the German automotive empire which bears his name.

The Ensign Grand Prix car was commissioned by von Opel from designer Morris Nunn, and he has incorporated some genuine innovations. The extremely low monocoque houses the side-mounted radiators and extends far behind the rear wheels into supports for the huge rear wing, while the fully enclosed engine and streamlined air box extend the tall, narrow cockpit into the wing area for effective surface development of the airfoil. The full-width aerodynamic nose is long and chisel-shaped.

The Ensign chassis is totally conventional, but the innovative body design seems to make it a highly competitive piece of hardware. Unfortunately for Mo Nunn, the inevitable and innumerable small problems which attend any new racing effort have kept the Ensign from competitive showings. The rightness of his initial Formula One design has yet to be conclusively proven.

Ferrari

Type: 312B3 **Engine:** Ferrari 312B, Flat-12 80.0x49.6mm, 2992cc; 485 hp at 12,500 rpm **Transmission:** Ferrari 5-speed transaxle **Chassis:** Monocoque **Wheelbase:** 97.4 in **Length:** 170.6 in **Width:** 80.9 in **Height:** 35.4 in **Track, F/R:** 63.9/63.1 in **Weight:** 1272 lbs **Wheels, F/R:** 11x13-in/17x13-in **Tires, F/R:** 9x20/14x26, Goodyear **Suspension, F/R:** Upper rocker arms, angled radius arms, lower wishbones, inboard coil spring/shock absorbers/ Upper radius arms, single upper links, reversed lower wishbones, outboard coil spring/shock absorbers **Brakes, F/R:** Outboard disc/Inboard disc, Lockheed **Fuel Capacity:** 55 gal

The Ferrari name has been associated with Grand Prix racing since 1919, in capacities ranging from driver to manufacturer. Ferrari won six World Championships between 1950 and 1964. Periodically in the decade that followed it seemed to be the team to beat, but internal management problems, engineering miscalculations and pure bad luck combined to help Ferrari defeat itself. In 1974, however, Ferrari returned to the forefront of Grand Prix competition.

The current cars are rather closely derived from the earlier 312s, but they have been much more successful. The 312B3 is the first monocoque Ferrari, using the engine as a stressed chassis member, with a large aluminum casting to mate the rear suspension to the engine itself. The original monocoque version was similar to that of the Lotus 72, with a long, pointed nose and side-mounted radiators. These worked poorly, and a larger cooling unit was secreted in the nose. Further modifications brought the radiators back to flank the cockpit, where they now serve very effectively.

Designed by Ferrari engineers Colombo and Rocchi, the 312B3 unfortunately also suffered from poor braking—a malady that has finally been corrected. The handling imprecision that plagued the cars in recent years has likewise been cured.

Unlike the BRM, which suffers from chronic engine deficiencies, Ferrari's Flat-12 produces demonstrably more horsepower than the

Ford Cosworth, but with unfortunately greater fuel consumption. This requires more fuel capacity, and hence greater bulk. A full cover for the low engine is a successful attempt at streamlining, for the Flat-12 allows a squashed rear deck by comparison to the tall Cosworth. The air intakes protrude as long scoops above the cam covers at the sides, while the oil coolers sit conspicuously exposed at the very rear of the chassis, above the transaxle.

The wide wing is mounted relatively low on the chassis, taking advantage of the pancake engine to achieve a more compact design. Inboard coil spring/shock absorbers leave little of the front suspension exposed to the air flow and constitute about the only unconventional feature of the chassis itself. In most other ways, the current Ferrari is a straightforward but surprisingly successful design, the finest standard-bearer in a decade from an old and proud house.

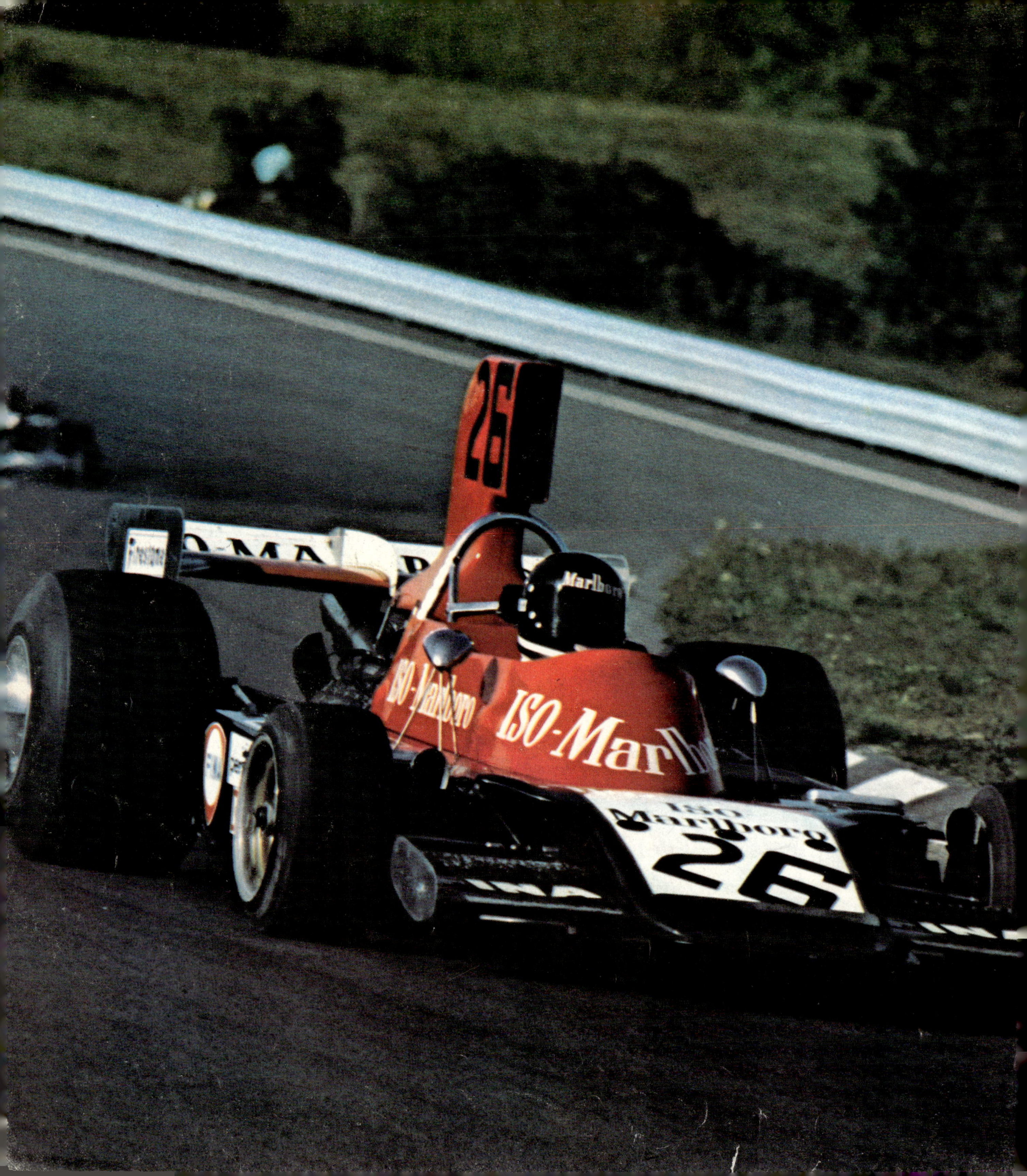
26
ISO-Marlboro
ISO
Marlboro
26

Frank Williams is the last of what was once a fairly extensive group of private entrants in Formula One. He has been running Grand Prix cars for years, but never with outstanding success or with first-rank drivers. His current racers are designed by Ron Tauranac, built by ISO-Rivolta—a large Italian machinery conglomerate—and sponsored by Marlboro cigarettes.

The angular monocoque chassis is similar to those on Dan Gurney's USAC Eagles, characterized by side-mounted radiators tucked far forward, close behind the front wheels. The tall, confining cockpit ends abruptly at the front of the engine, and the long, elevated wing is carried on a single fabricated boom mounted to the rear of the Ford Cosworth.

In all other respects, the ISO is a very conventional design that has been raced by a number of drivers with little success. At least some of its failures, however, can be blamed on the unusual radiator placement. This has never functioned properly, and overheating—particularly on high-speed tracks—has been a constant annoyance.

ISO

Type: IR **Engine:** Ford Cosworth DFV, V-8 85.6x64.8mm, 2993cc; 450 hp at 11,000 rpm
Transmission: Hewland FG400A 5-speed transaxle **Chassis:** Monocoque
Wheelbase: 98 in **Length:** 173.8 in
Width: 77 in **Height:** 37 in
Track, F/R: 62.0/60.0 in **Weight:** 1275 lbs
Wheels, F/R: 11x13-in/17x13-in
Tires, F/R: 10x20/17x26, Firestone
Suspension, F/R: Upper and lower wishbones, outboard coil spring/shock absorbers/Twin radius arms, single upper links, double lower links, outboard coil spring/shock absorbers
Brakes, F/R: Outboard disc/Inboard disc, Lockheed **Fuel Capacity:** 41 gal

JPS Lotus

In the last ten years, Lotus has won the International Cup for Formula One Manufacturers five times, making Colin Chapman's efficient organization the most overwhelmingly successful in modern Grand Prix racing. Chapman has been producing winning designs since his college days in the late Forties, although he now acts as the team chief and owner rather than designer and tester. Over a period of twenty years, Lotus racers have built up a reputation as fast, innovative designs with an unfortunate tendency toward fragility. Some drivers have refused to work for Chapman because of this, but those who do drive for Lotus often win.

The winningest Lotus Grand Prix car is the Lotus 72D. Designed by the brilliant British engineer Maurice Phillippe, the Lotus 72 is now considered perhaps the most significant car to be produced since Formula One designers discovered the mid-engine chassis in the late Fifties. In 1970, the Lotus 72 won a posthumous World Championship for Jochen Rindt in the first year of its appearance. After a training season, it won another for Emerson Fittipaldi in 1972.

The most superficially copied of current racers, the Lotus 72 is also the most unconventional. It was the first to utilize side-mounted radiators in order to achieve a sharply aerodynamic shovel nose, the only Formula One car to use a variable-rate torsion bar suspension at both front and rear and the first in modern history to incorporate inboard shaft-driven front disc brakes. Unlike the cars of most other teams, it has remained substantially the same for five racing seasons, attesting to the rightness of the original design. In 1973 the monocoque was widened adjacent to the cockpit to incorporate the mandatory deformable protective structure, but otherwise the only real changes have been minor fiddles to the suspension in 1971.

Maurice Phillippe's ideas have had an astounding influence on other designers. The current McLaren is a near copy of the Lotus 72, and the American Shadow appears very similar. In Formula 5000, the current Lola was clearly inspired by Phillippe's design, while McLarens and Eagles for USAC National Championship racing are also similar. Phillippe switched to the Vels-Parnelli USAC team in 1971, and his first Parnelli oval-track racer was also an obvious and logical derivation of his own successful Lotus 72.

Type: 72D **Engine:** Ford Cosworth DFV, V-8 85.6x64.8mm, 2993cc; 460 hp at 10,500 rpm **Transmission:** Hewland FG400A 5-speed transaxle **Chassis:** Monocoque **Wheelbase:** 100 in **Length:** 195 in **Width:** 75.5 in **Height:** 36 in **Track, F/R:** 58.0/61.0 in **Weight:** 1346 lbs **Wheels, F/R:** 10x13-in/17x13-in **Tires, F/R:** 9x20/14x26, Goodyear **Suspension, F/R:** Upper and lower wishbones, torsion bars/ Twin radius arms, single upper links, double lower links, torsion bars **Brakes, F/R:** Inboard disc/Inboard disc, Girling **Fuel Capacity:** 39 gal

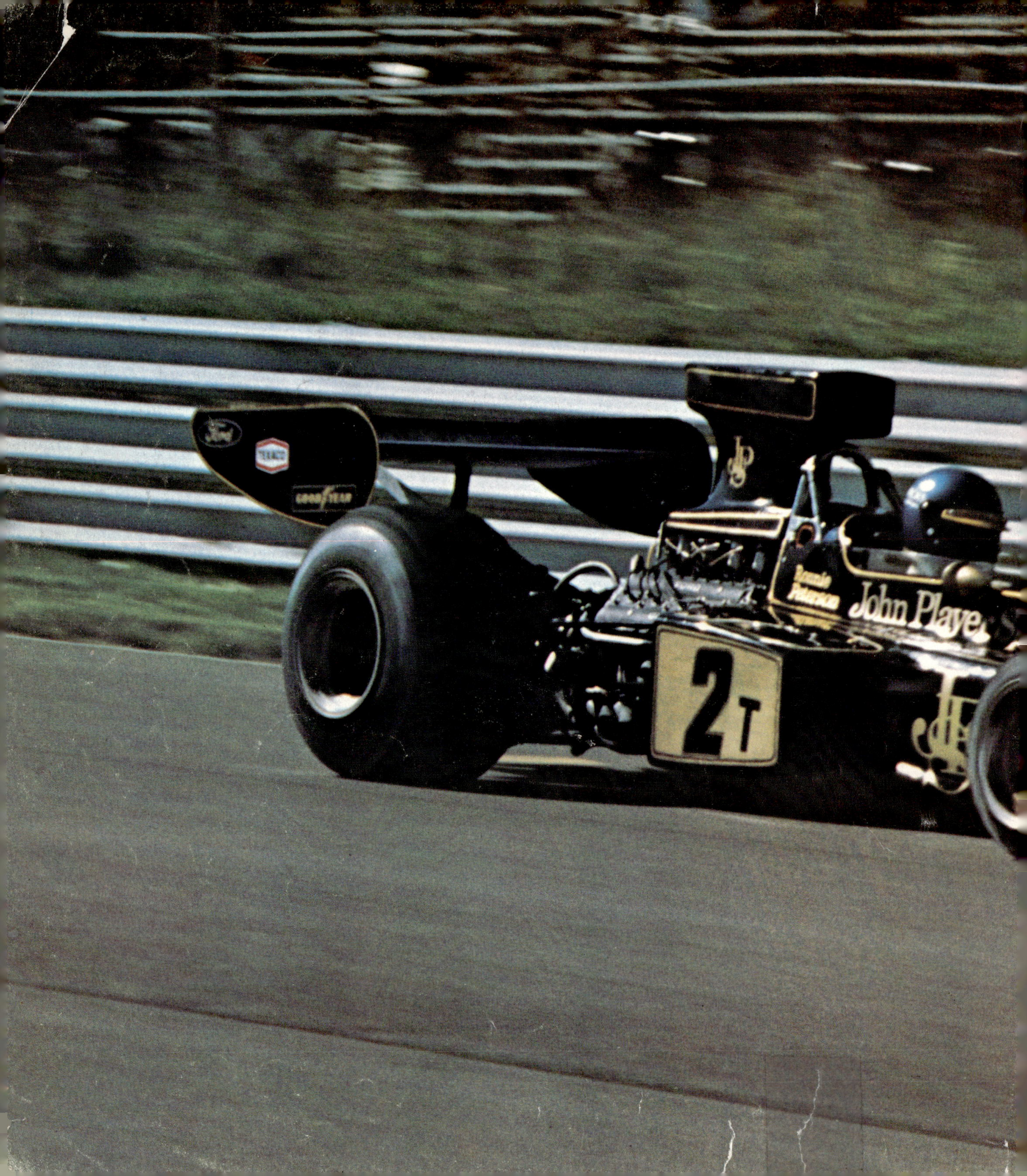

2T
John Player

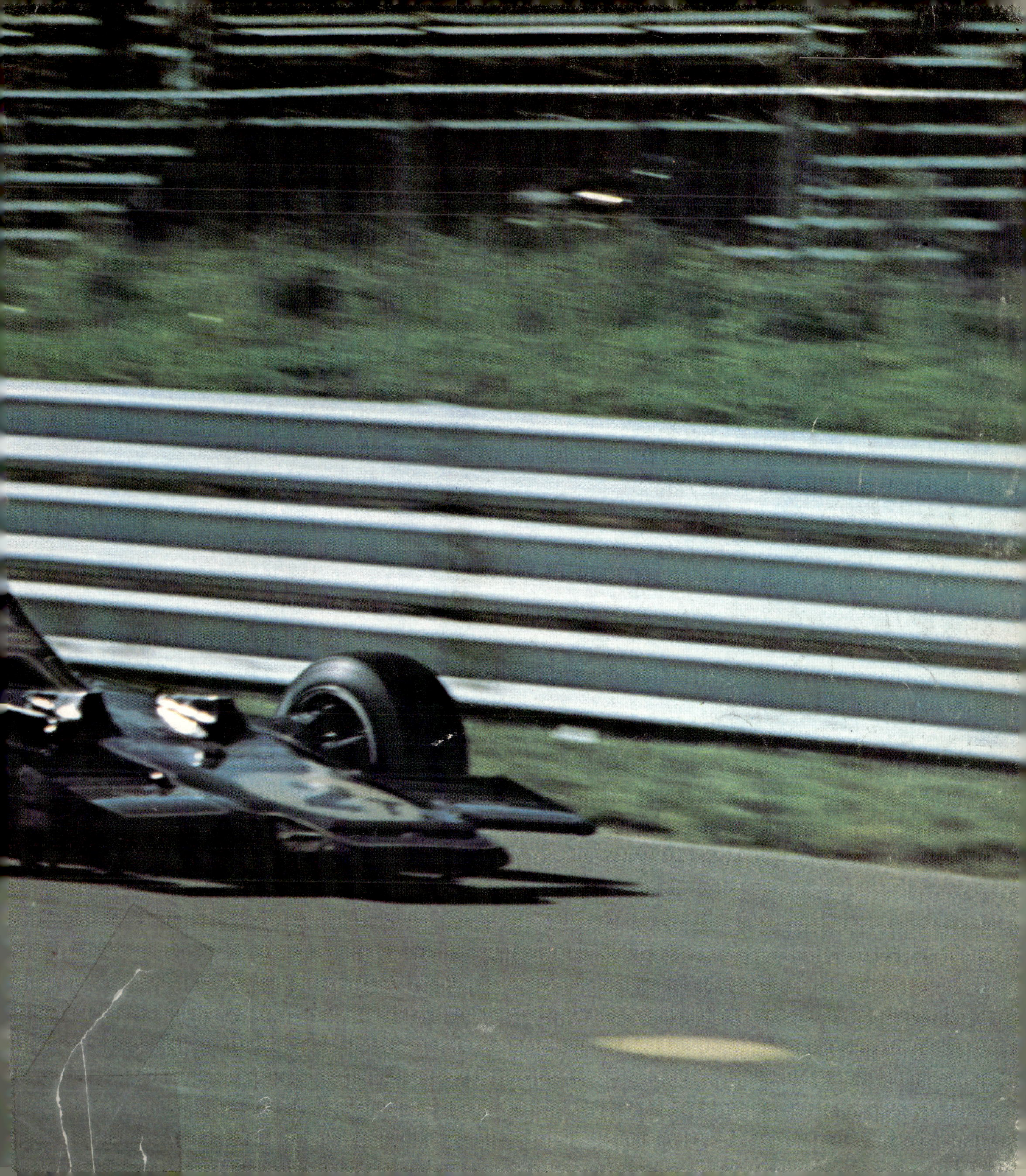

March

An all-new organization, March first appeared in 1970 with experienced and respected personnel but overly ambitious plans for the construction of Formula cars and sports racers for nearly all classes. The firm initially enjoyed the backing of STP and sold cars to Ken Tyrrell for Jackie Stewart's use before the Tyrrell itself appeared.

As dolefully predicted from the start, March was vastly overextended, and long-suffering driver Chris Amon was only one of the big names caught out by the subsequent fiasco. In later years, March has been content to field one car under STP auspices, while selling modified versions to independent teams.

The current March Grand Prix car is the smallest of the competitors, for the very good reason that it is an expanded and strengthened Formula Two car rather than a design intended from the outset for Formula One. The main points of interest are the extremely short wheelbase coupled with a very wide section through the monocoque chassis. The monocoque incorporates ducting for the side-mounted radiators, and different styles of air boxes have been tried. All are extremely tall, to rise above the disturbed air near the surface of the body. In addition, each of the three regularly raced cars has appeared with at least one version of a modified Tyrrell-type nose. A well-prepared March can be a very competitive vehicle, but on the whole, March has failed to live up to its initial promise.

Type: 731 **Engine:** Ford Cosworth DFV, V-8 85.6x64.8mm, 2993cc; 450 hp at 10,000 rpm **Transmission:** Hewland FG400A 5-speed transaxle **Chassis:** Monocoque
Wheelbase: 93 in **Length:** 157 in
Width: 78.5 in **Height:** 36 in
Track, F/R: 61.5/61.5 in **Weight:** 1268 lbs
Wheels, F/R: 11x13-in/17x13-in
Tires, F/R: 10x20/17x26, Goodyear
Suspension, F/R: Upper and lower wishbones, outboard coil spring/shock absorbers/Twin radius arms, single upper links, lower wishbones, outboard coil spring/shock absorbers
Brakes, F/R: Outboard disc/Inboard disc, Girling or Lockheed **Fuel Capacity:** 38 gal

McLaren

Bruce McLaren Motor Racing has always taken a rather scattergun approach to development, designing cars for the Can-Am and USAC as well as for Formula One. The firm has also prepared customer cars in addition to team vehicles. This dispersion of energies has not affected McLaren's performance in the Can-Am and USAC; indeed, McLaren cars have dominated those series in past seasons. In 1973, the Penske Porsches drove McLaren out of the Can-Am, but McLaren's Gordon Coppuck-designed M16 continues to be very competitive in USAC National Championship racing.

McLaren began building cars for Formula One in 1966 and has

always fielded a formidable team without achieving the expected success. The M23 McLaren is patterned after the Lotus 72—as is the USAC McLaren M16C—and, for a period late in the 1973 season, appeared to be the car to beat before it faded in the face of Tyrrell and JPS-Lotus competition.

An angular wedge like the Lotus, the McLaren also uses side-mounted radiators in conjunction with a shovel nose. Unlike the Lotus 72, however, the front brakes are mounted out in the wheels. The front coil spring/shock absorbers are mounted horizontally within the body, an aerodynamic trick shared with McLaren's own USAC racer. The rear wing is mounted further back than usual on a single fabricated central support, but in other respects the McLaren M23 represents a conventional use of the Ford Cosworth DFV wrapped in a Lotus-inspired package.

Type: M23 **Engine:** Ford Cosworth DFV, V-8 85.6x64.8mm, 2993cc; 460 hp at 10,000 rpm
Transmission: Hewland FG400A 5-speed transaxle **Chassis:** Monocoque
Wheelbase: 101 in **Length:** 160 in
Width: 82 in **Height:** 33 in
Track, F/R: 65.5/62.5 in **Weight:** 1270 lbs
Wheels, F/R: 11x13-in/17x13-in
Tires, F/R: 10x20/17x26, Goodyear
Suspension, F/R: Upper rocker arms, lower wishbones, inboard coil spring/shock absorbers/Twin radius arms, single upper links, lower wishbones, outboard coil spring/shock absorbers
Brakes, F/R: Outboard disc/Inboard disc, Lockheed **Fuel Capacity:** 42 gal

Embassy
RACING
ith Graham Hill
Embassy
Embassy
RACING
Esso
GOODYEAR
12
Esso
GOODYEAR

American fabricator Don Nichols has been building racing cars for years, including the wildly innovative but spectacularly unsuccessful original Shadow Can-Am car designed by Trevor Harris. Tony Southgate—designer of the Grand Prix BRM as well—is the current creator of Shadows. Perhaps not as original as Harris, Southgate has been demonstrably more successful.

Until 1973, when the first Shadow Formula One appeared, Nichols entered cars only in the Can-Am—intriguing, extremely low Group Seven beasts, never really competitive with the prevailing McLarens or Porsches. The Grand Prix contender, however, enjoyed some encouraging success at the very beginning. Since then, though, the Shadow has been nothing more than a very pretty addition to the middle of Formula One grids.

The Shadows are always well prepared, and the organization—headquartered in England although sponsored by an American oil company—has been thoroughly competent. And the vehicle seems to be a basically sound design. It resembles the Lotus 72 and McLaren M23 quite closely, with a very clean aerodynamic body. There is a fully streamlined engine cover with tall air box, side-mounted radiators and a very low, sharply pointed nose which droops over the front suspension. But beneath the fascinating and attractive body there lies a conventional monocoque chassis.

Shadow

Type: DN1 **Engine:** Ford Cosworth DFV, V-8 85.6x64.8mm, 2993cc; 430 hp at 10,000 rpm
Transmission: Hewland FG400A 5-speed transaxle **Chassis:** Monocoque
Wheelbase: 100 in **Length:** 175 in
Width: 77 in **Height:** 46.5 in
Track, F/R: 61.0/60.0 in **Weight:** 1265 lbs
Wheels, F/R: 12x13-in/17x13-in
Tires, F/R: 10x20/17x26, Goodyear
Suspension, F/R: Upper and lower wishbones, outboard coil spring/shock absorbers/Single radius arms, single upper links, lower wishbones, outboard coil spring/shock absorbers
Brakes, F/R: Outboard disc/Inboard disc, Lockheed **Fuel Capacity:** 42 gal

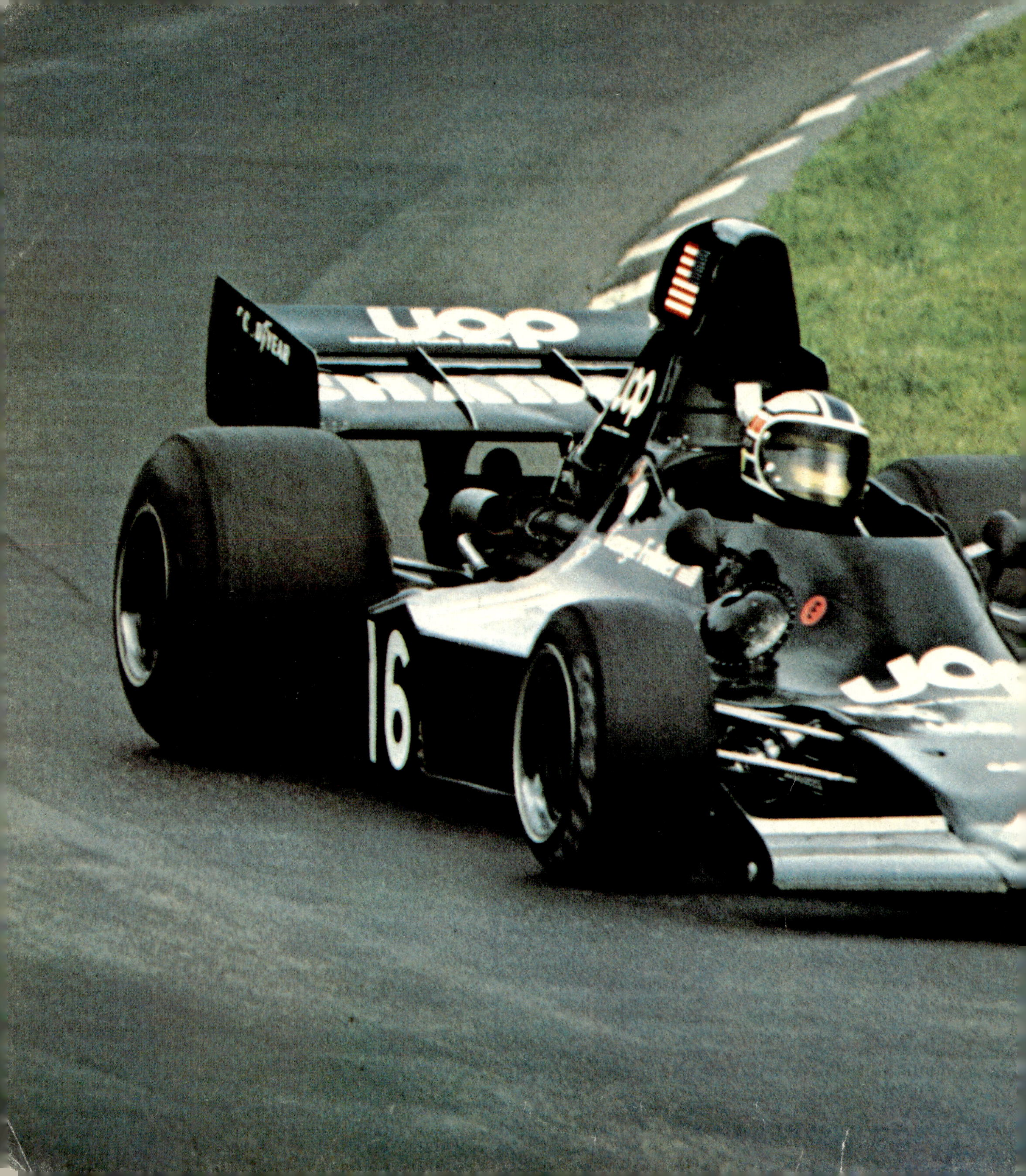
uop
16
uop

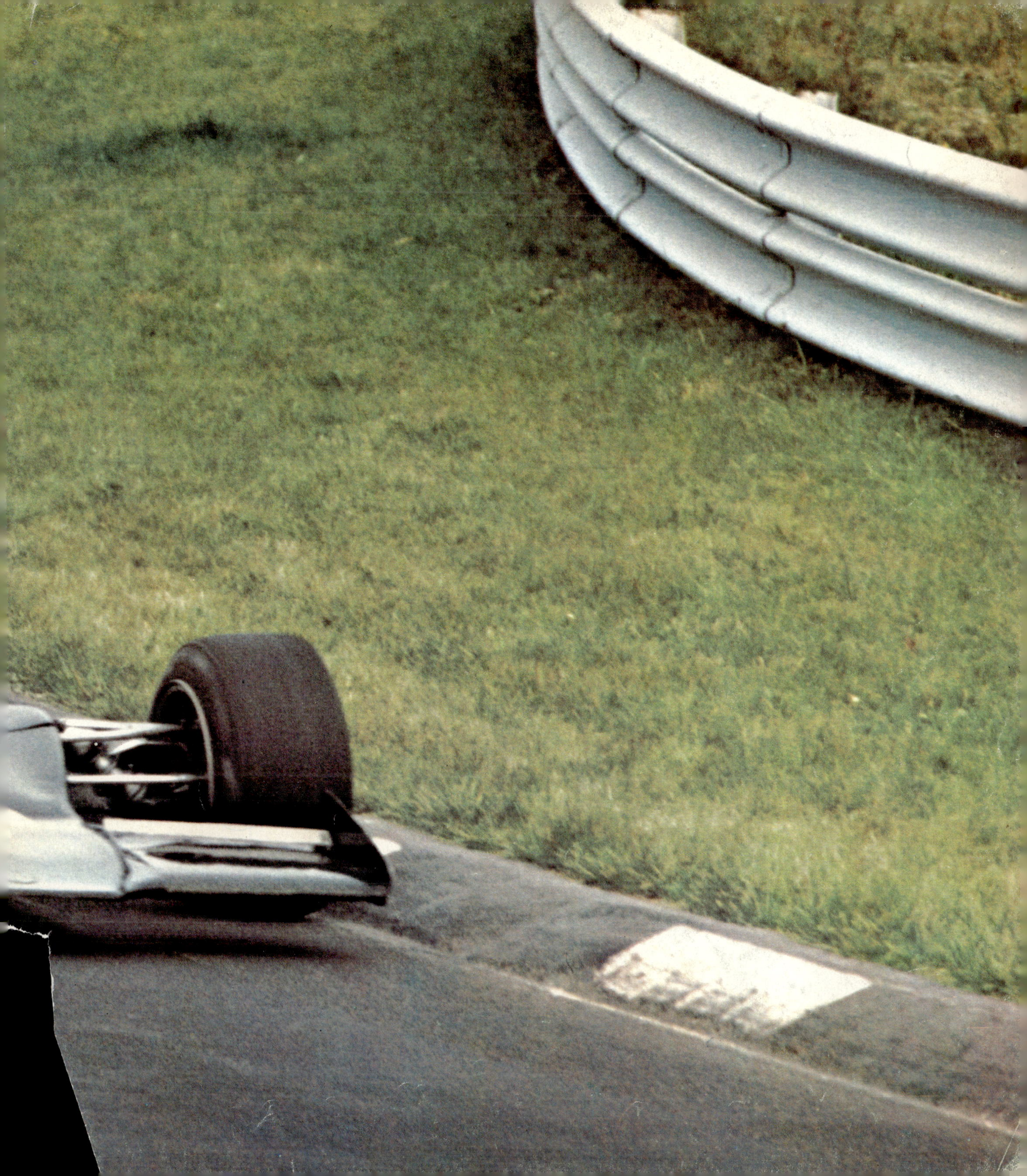

Surtees

Type: TS14A **Engine:** Ford Cosworth DFV, V-8 85.6x64.8mm, 2993cc; 450 hp at 10,500 rpm
Transmission: Hewland FG400A 5-speed transaxle **Chassis:** Monocoque
Wheelbase: 102 in **Length:** 170 in
Width: 78 in **Height:** 39 in
Track, F/R: 60.0/62.5 in **Weight:** 1265 lbs
Wheels, F/R: 10x13-in/17x13-in
Tires, F/R: 10x20/16x26, Firestone
Suspension, F/R: Upper and lower wishbones, outboard coil spring/shock absorbers/Twin radius arms, single upper links, lower wishbones, outboard coil spring/shock absorbers
Brakes, F/R: Outboard disc/Inboard disc, Lockheed **Fuel Capacity:** 42 gal

Former World Champion John Surtees is the only owner/builder/driver left in Formula One. Although he ostensibly retired from active competition in 1971, Surtees still does some of his own development driving. He usually fields three cars, one of which is sponsored by the British Brooke Bond grocery products company, allied with Formula One fixture Rob Walker. Surtees has been very successful in Formula Two, but the Grand Prix cars have never shown much promise, despite dedicated and thorough testing proven design concepts by their very knowledgeable creator.

A conventional Ford Cosworth chassis, the Surtees is distinguished by the longest wheelbase on any current Grand Prix car features a full-width nose with supplementary vertical fins and a very rounded contour which drops close to the pavement. The radiators, mounted near the rear wheel à la Lotus 72, flank the driver. The most unusual design features are the NACA ducts, which admit air to the upper surfaces of the radiator sponsons rather than to the side as is more common in current Formula One machinery. The distinctive air box rises high above the cockpit, and the large two-piece rear wing is carried on tubular supports from the engine and transaxle. The cockpit is narrow and angular, with a chisel-shaped leading edge. This mates abruptly with the flat-topped, slab-sided monocoque to produce a body of extreme angularity.

Tyrrell

Ken Tyrrell, like Rob Walker and Frank Williams, started out as a gentleman-entrant who provided rides for unknown but promising drivers. Tyrrell sponsored Jackie Stewart in Formula Three and Formula Two before Stewart's years with BRM in Formula One. He entered Formula One only in 1968, when Stewart felt ready for a more stable situation than existed at BRM. At that point, Tyrrell entered Matra and later March chassis, powered by Ford Cosworths. In 1970, after Stewart's World Championship for Matra, Derek Gardner designed the first Tyrrell for what had by then become far more than a mere private entrant's campaign.

The latest Tyrrell designed by Gardner has a rather angular monocoque incorporating the mandatory deformable structure. It is built with a very short wheelbase by current standards. Gardner introduced the wide and aerodynamic type of "sports car" nose on an earlier model, and it has been copied on nearly all those cars which are not derived from the equally innovative Lotus 72. Brabham, BRM, March, Surtees and Ensign all use similar noses in Formula One, while nearly all Formula Two and Formula 5000 competitors ride behind some version of the Derek Gardner snout. There has of course been cross-influence with the other successful school of Formula One design derived from Maurice Phillippe's pioneering work for Colin Chapman, and inboard front disc brakes with raised exhaust scoops testify to the influence of the Lotus 72 on the current Tyrrell model 006/2.

The remainder of the car is a compact package with good reliability—except for the inboard front brakes, which suffered chronic cooling problems for more than one season. The huge air box is perched conspicuously over the engine, its distinctive banana shape cut short at the rear. The rear wing is mounted separately on tubular struts, while the chassis curves in dramatically behind the cockpit and leaves the sides and top of the Ford Cosworth exposed to the airstream. And the tall Tyrrell cockpit is cut so closely to the driver that an optional version with teardrop-shaped reliefs for arms and elbows has been fitted.

The Tyrrell organization has one of the most enviable records in the 3-liter formula, having built its first car for the 1970 season and won the World Championship in 1971 and 1973. Much of its success was due to the inspired driving of Jackie Stewart, but the cars were always cleverly designed, carefully built, perfectly prepared, well-tested and superlatively managed.

Type: 006/2 **Engine:** Ford Cosworth DFV, V-8 85.6x64.8mm, 2993cc; 465 hp at 10,200 rpm
Transmission: Hewland FG400A 5-speed transaxle **Chassis:** Monocoque
Wheelbase: 94 in **Length:** 165 in
Width: 81.8 in **Height:** 40 in
Track, F/R: 63.6/64.8 in **Weight:** 1340 lbs
Wheels, F/R: 10x13-in/17x13-in
Tires, F/R: 10x20/17x26, Goodyear
Suspension, F/R: Upper and lower fabricated links, outboard coil spring/shock absorbers/Twin radius arms, single upper links, double lower links, outboard coil spring/shock absorbers
Brakes, F/R: Inboard disc/Inboard disc, Lockheed **Fuel Capacity:** 41 gal